The Art of African Masks

The Art of African Masks

Exploring Cultural Traditions

BY CAROL FINLEY

LERNER PUBLICATIONS COMPANY ■ MINNEAPOLIS

Introduction
to Masks

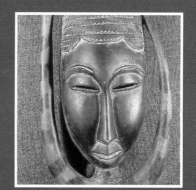

PEOPLE OF MANY CULTURES—BOTH RECENT
and ancient—have made masks. Gold, stone, wood, bark, copper, bronze, tin, clay, feathers, and ivory are some of the materials used in mask making. Some masks are also decorated with colors, patterns, and textures. The resulting piece might look fierce, festive, or solemn. Some masks are one part of an elaborate costume.

You can appreciate the appearance of a mask even if you know nothing about its meaning. But if you can learn how and why the mask was used, you can increase your appreciation of it and understand the cultural traditions of the people that made it.

Sometimes even experts can't know the exact function of a particular mask because there are no records of its original use. What they can do is make suggestions and guesses regarding the intentions of the artist and the wearer. The meaning of the mask and the mask ceremony remain a mystery to the outsider. In the modern world, people might collect masks, and museums might display them, but originally the masks had a specific purpose. They were much more than decorative art objects.

People have used masks for many reasons. For example, actors from ancient Greece and Rome played some roles wearing masks. This was to facilitate the actor's impersonation of the character. The Japanese and Chinese still use elaborate masks in some of their traditional theater. Although in Western society most actors do not use masks in theater anymore, a pair of

Dogon dancers perform an ancestral ceremony in Mali.

masks, one comic and one tragic, have become a widely recognized symbol of drama.

People make masks for many other reasons, too. Tibetans hang brightly colored, fierce-looking masks to scare away demons. The Hopi, a Native American tribe in the southwestern United States, make *kachinas*, masks representing helpful spirits. The ancient Egyptians made masks that covered their mummies. Many people still wear masks at events such as Halloween, Carnival, and Mardi Gras. Have you ever worn a mask? What was the mask like and why did you wear it?

chapter one

Masks of
Africa

Masks are used in many traditional dances. A Dobon dancer in Mali participates in a Dama ceremony, which eases passage to the afterlife, *left. Below,* men perform a traditional dance in Togo.

MASK MAKING IS A MAJOR TRADITION IN West and Central Africa. (See map on page 22.) Many people in African countries use masks for ceremonial and religious purposes. Masks can represent entities such as spirits, legendary animals, or mythological beings. Sometimes people wear masks with a costume as part of a ritual or performance. Secret societies also use masks in their rites and initiations.

Masks often make a strong visual impression. When you look at masks in an art museum, you recognize them as stunning artistic achievements, but you do not see them in their intended context. When worn as part of a costume by a person dancing to music, a mask takes on a powerful symbolic meaning that is lost when it is viewed alone. Most viewers can understand only a fraction of the meaning a mask has within the culture of a particular society.

The Function of the African Mask

The purpose of a mask is not only to conceal the identity of the wearer. The mask actually creates a new identity—one from the spirit world. Many Africans use masks in private initiations, in the rituals of secret societies, and in coming-of-age ceremonies. People use masks in public ceremonies, such as funerals, harvest celebrations, acts of thanksgiving, and in other rituals. And some societies also use masks to ensure fertility and abundance of crops and animals.

An adze is a cutting tool that has a thin, arched blade set at a right angle to the handle. It is used chiefly for shaping wood.

Masks are considered vessels of spiritual power, but they can also be used to teach values. In a masked dance, for example, lessons and morals might be taught. Many mask-making African societies did not have a written language. Masks and performances were one way for them to pass on their heritage.

How Masks Were Made

Many of the artists who carved masks were also farmers or blacksmiths. The carver often learned the craft from a parent or during an apprenticeship with an established artist.

Wood is the most common material used for making African masks. Most of the masks available for study are no more than 100 years old, because wood rarely lasts longer than that in a tropical climate. Although some masks and costumes are passed down through generations, others are made for a particular occasion and are not preserved.

The wood used for mask making comes from local forests and is carved with an adze, a cutting tool that has a thin, arched blade set at a right angle to the handle. The adze—used mainly for shaping wood—is the carver's chief tool. A carver often uses two or three of them with slightly differing sizes and shapes. Fine detail is put in later with a small knife. The carver might finish all the carving with one knife after roughly adzing the block of wood to the right shape and size. The carver works seated on the ground, often holding the block of wood in position with his feet. Besides wood, mask makers also use ivory, metals, and beads. Sometimes the mask maker might further decorate the mask by painting it or attaching other materials, such as feathers, horns, or fiber to it. Carvers believed that the tools they used had special powers and that the wood itself housed a living spirit. A priest might consecrate a finished mask to give it the desired spiritual quality.

Masks are not portraits of people. The shape of a mask is traditional and not subject to the stylistic taste of its maker. Mask makers generally conform to existing models of

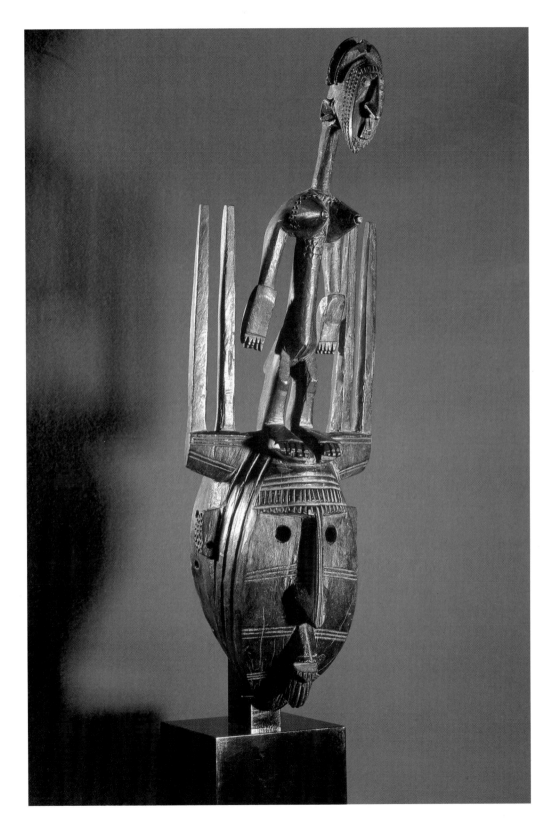

A Bamana dance mask with a human figure on top, from Mali

This wooden shoulder mask from the Baga people in Guinea is 56 inches high.

masks rather than create their own designs. A design that had evidently pleased the spirits in the past is usually followed carefully. The similarity allows the desired spirit to recognize the mask and come to dwell in it.

A new mask might be inspired by an image seen in a dream. The dreamer would present this information to the elders of the society, and they would decide if the mask should be carved. A mask usually has its own appointed dancer, an appointment that might last several decades and then remain in the same line of descent from one generation to another.

Types of Masks

African masks can be designed to cover the head, cover just the face, or be used as a headdress that is attached to the top of the head. Not all masks are life-size. They can be gigantic or very small. The large and life-size masks are used in public performances and private rituals. The small masks are used as

Dogon dancers in an ancestral ceremony in Mali

charms or amulets to cure illness and to offer protection during work or travel. Sometimes small masks are made as miniature copies of larger masks.

The features on a mask can be human, animal, or a combination of the two. The expressions range from terrifying to serene. The examples of masks in this book will give you an idea of the range of imagery, technique, and style found in the masks of Africa.

chapter two

Regions of
Mask-Making
Cultures

The Treichville market in Abidjan, Ivory Coast, attracts many shoppers, *below.*

Bustling fishing boats crowd the harbor in Elmina, Ghana, *above,* and people stroll a quiet street in N'Djamena, the capital city of Chad, *right.*

AFRICA IS A VAST LAND. IT IS THE SECOND largest continent on earth. The diverse population—706 million people—is made up of more than 1,000 different ethnic groups. The exact number is unknown because of the difficulty of defining precisely what makes up an ethnic group. Some groups overlap, and specific information about others is sometimes scarce. More than 1,000 languages are spoken in Africa, which has over 50 independent countries.

Each ethnic group has its own history, customs, and culture. Although there are some similarities in religion and ritual throughout Africa, there are also wide-ranging differences in cultural traditions. Masks were made mainly by settled agricultural groups, such as those living in western and central Africa, and masks are part of the tradition of those cultural groups. The traditional way of life and beliefs have, to some extent, disappeared in Africa. Colonialism, the spread of Islam and Christianity, and the advent of modern governments have all contributed to the decline of the earlier, traditional way of life. Africa, like every other place, changes with time. The masking tradition, like many of the masks shown in this book, for the most part belongs to an earlier, now vanishing, age.

Great stylistic diversity exists in African art, which reflects the complex array of different African cultures. The major mask-making societies are south of the Sahara Desert and span from Guinea on the Atlantic Coast, west to Cameroon, and then southwest through the Democratic Republic of the

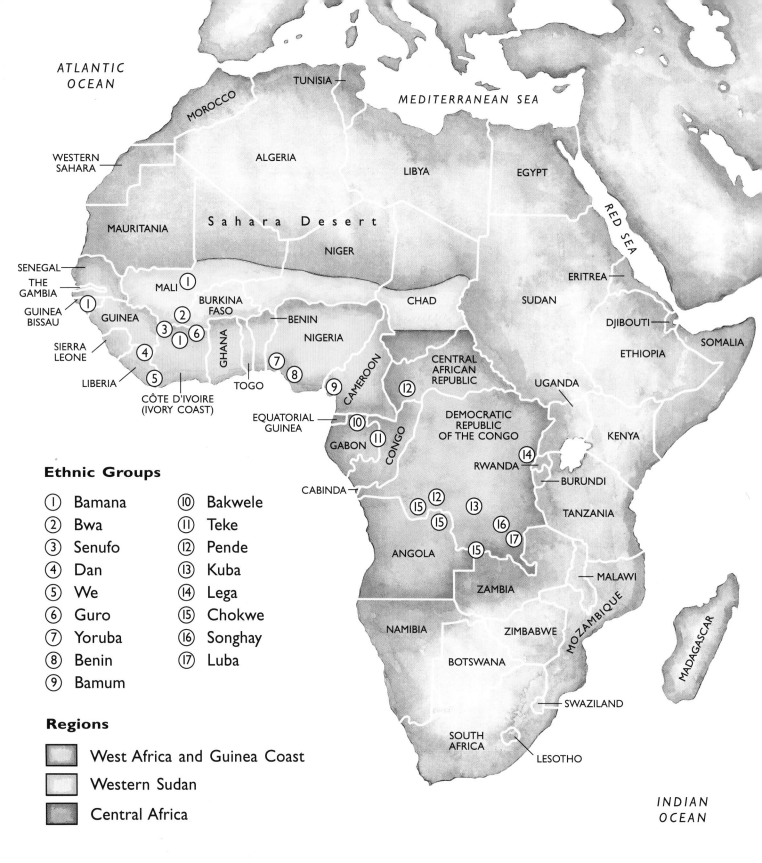

ATLANTIC OCEAN

MEDITERRANEAN SEA

TUNISIA

MOROCCO

ALGERIA

LIBYA

EGYPT

WESTERN SAHARA

MAURITANIA

Sahara Desert

NIGER

RED SEA

SENEGAL
THE GAMBIA
GUINEA BISSAU

MALI ①

BURKINA FASO

CHAD

SUDAN

ERITREA

GUINEA

②

③ ⑥

①

BENIN

NIGERIA

DJIBOUTI

SIERRA LEONE

④

GHANA

CENTRAL AFRICAN REPUBLIC

ETHIOPIA

SOMALIA

LIBERIA

⑤

⑦

⑧

CÔTE D'IVOIRE (IVORY COAST)

TOGO

⑨

CAMEROON

⑫

DEMOCRATIC REPUBLIC OF THE CONGO

UGANDA

KENYA

EQUATORIAL GUINEA

⑩

GABON

⑪

CONGO

RWANDA

⑭

BURUNDI

CABINDA

⑮

⑫

⑬

TANZANIA

⑮

⑯

⑰

ANGOLA

⑮

MALAWI

ZAMBIA

MOZAMBIQUE

MADAGASCAR

NAMIBIA

ZIMBABWE

BOTSWANA

SWAZILAND

SOUTH AFRICA

LESOTHO

INDIAN OCEAN

Ethnic Groups

① Bamana
② Bwa
③ Senufo
④ Dan
⑤ We
⑥ Guro
⑦ Yoruba
⑧ Benin
⑨ Bamum

⑩ Bakwele
⑪ Teke
⑫ Pende
⑬ Kuba
⑭ Lega
⑮ Chokwe
⑯ Songhay
⑰ Luba

Regions

West Africa and Guinea Coast

Western Sudan

Central Africa

In a millet field in Chad, a boy pulls the oxen while his mother drives the plow and his sister goads the animals.

Congo. Historians, for convenience and because of some stylistic and cultural similarities, have grouped the mask-making societies into various regions for study and discussion. This book divides the major mask-making societies into three areas: the Western Sudan, the Guinea Coast, and Central Africa. This book includes masks from each of these areas.

The Western Sudan

The area called the Western Sudan does not refer to the country of Sudan, but to an area south of the Sahara Desert. This grassy, tree-covered region includes the countries of Mali, Burkina Faso, Niger, and Chad.

The northern part of this region, bordering the Sahara, has a semiarid climate. Many people in this area have traditionally been cattle herders and camel breeders. In the southern sections, however, the savanna (grasslands) and woodlands are more suitable for farming. The major crops are millet (a grain), sorghum (tropical grasses), cowpeas, and cotton.

The Western Sudan is the site of some of Africa's earliest cities and most powerful empires. Flourishing trade and commerce shaped the history of this area. Trade routes with the north were established as early as the eighth century, and through the centuries active trade took place with North Africa, the

Figure 1
Bamana
*Antelope
Headdresses*

Mediterranean, and the Near East. Trade goods, which included gold, ivory, iron bars, leather, and sorghum, were usually transported by camel.

Many cultural groups populate the Western Sudan region. They use masks in agricultural rites, funeral rites, seasonal celebrations, and initiations into private associations.

The Bamana Culture

The Bamana people are primarily an agricultural society who live throughout Mali and in parts of Ivory Coast and Guinea-Bissau. With more than three million people, they are the most populous ethnic group in Mali. The majority of the Bamana people have converted to Islam, but the traditional religion and rituals are still practiced in the rural areas. There, the Bamana practice cooperative farming.

They use a pair of carved antelope figures as headdresses in agricultural ceremonies.

These carved, wooden antelope figures (**figure 1**) are fastened to a cap and worn on top of the head. Long strands of black-dyed fiber hang down and cover the body of the wearer. These fiber strands represent the rain that falls on the Bamana's crops.

The antelope depicted is a legendary figure, called *Tyi Wara,* who taught the Bamana how to farm. This type of headdress would be used in ceremonies and feasts during the planting and harvesting seasons by farmers who belong to the Tyi Wara association.

The headdresses are carved in pairs—one male and one female. The male antelope is the larger figure on the right, shown here with an openwork pattern on the mane. The female antelope, on the left, carries a baby on her back. The horn of the antelope represents

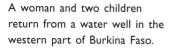

A woman and two children return from a water well in the western part of Burkina Faso.

the planted grain sprouting through the earth. A pair of dancers wore these headdresses, imitating the leaps of the antelope to honor the legendary Tyi Wara and to ensure a successful planting season.

The Bamana also make a face mask with an antelope headdress that is used in initiation rites and other masks that are used by their various associations.

The Bwa Culture

The Bwa live in Burkina Faso and Mali. They are fiercely independent people who have resisted foreign intervention. The Bwa share many beliefs and traditions with the Bobo, who live in the same area. The majority of their populations continue to observe the traditional religious and cultural practices. Both cultures believe in a supreme god called Dwo, and both cultures are based on agriculture. They grow sorghum, millet, and cotton. The Bwa people also make and sell fabric from cotton they dye and weave.

The Bwa make a range of masks carved from wood and painted with geometric shapes and patterns. Some of these masks—called plank masks—are six or seven feet high. They are worn during funeral ceremonies and planting and harvesting rituals.

This Bwa mask (**figure 2**) is called a hawk mask. Instead of being constructed vertically to be very high, this mask is made to be very wide. The dancer who wears it uses a spiral motion to twist his head so the mask appears to spin. The eyes and mouth of the mask are circular, and a horn or antler juts out of the forehead. The geometric pattern,

Figure 2, Bwa, *Hawk Mask*

made up of triangles, is painted red, black, and white.

Some Bwa masks represent supernatural flying creatures that live in the bush. These benevolent spirits provide protection and blessings to the families who possess their particular masks.

The Senufo Culture

The Senufo are an ethnic group of more than one million people who live in the area where Ivory Coast, Mali, and Burkina Faso meet. They are primarily subsistence farmers, growing crops that include cotton, bananas, rice, corn, and peanuts. Although many Senufo are converting to Islam, many remain faithful to their traditional belief system.

Secret associations for men and women, called *poro* and *sandogo*, are an important as-

Two Senufo dancers walk together in the village of Boundali, Ivory Coast, *above*. In Niger, where the desert meets the Niger River, most village activities take place along the riverbank, *left*.

pect of their society. These secret associations have various grades or levels. Members are initiated into a particular level depending on their age, status, and achievement. Masks are used in the ceremonies of the secret associations and in the performance of burial rites.

The Senufo are known for their music and art traditions. Wood-carvers, who make masks and sculpture, follow a long apprenticeship of seven to eight years to learn the craft from established artists. Senufo carving is smooth and rounded, giving the impression of a series of curves flowing forward and downward. This carved wood mask **(figure 3)** is called a *Kpele* mask. It is a complex work of art with a distinct vitality. The face is carved in an oval shape with a pointed chin and a mouth showing teeth—characteristic features of Senufo masks.

On top of this mask is a headdress shaped like a bird. The sides and top of the mask are decorated with graceful curved appendages.

Figure 3
Senufo
Kpele Mask

The long appendages coming down from the top of the mask might represent hair or animal horns. Sacrificial marks—a kind of tattoo—are carved into the cheeks and forehead of the mask, and leglike projections jut out from the bottom.

This mask can be worn with a costume of long fibers and knotted rope. It is used at elaborate funerals organized by members of the poro association.

West Africa and the Guinea Coast

The area called West Africa and the Guinea Coast—along the coast of the Atlantic Ocean—stretches from Senegal to Cameroon and includes the nations of Guinea, Sierra Leone, Liberia, Ivory Coast, Ghana, Togo, Benin, and Nigeria. The land is varied and ranges from swamp and dense, tropical rain forests to more open savanna landscapes with woodlands mixed with tall grasses and rolling hills. Early trade in this region took place over land through trade routes heading north and by sea from coastal ports.

In the western portion of the Guinea Coast, masks are used in initiations and in the rites of men's and women's secret associations. To the peoples of the eastern Guinea Coast, masks represent spirits and are used for

At Elmina, Ghana's second largest port, fishermen work from traditional canoes.

Children sell produce in the village of Kong, Ivory Coast.

rituals and celebrations. Cultural groups in this region include the Dan, We, Guro, Benin, Yoruba, and Bamum.

The Dan Culture

The Dan live in northern Liberia and western Ivory Coast. They farm their land, raising goats and chickens and growing nuts, fruits, rice, and cotton. They also hunt game and fish. Some Dan men leave their villages to work seasonally as laborers in other areas.

This society has a reputation for having fierce warriors, feared by neighboring societies. The Dan believe the world has two realms. One is made up of the villages where humans live, and the other is the forest—home to wild animals and bush spirits.

given to Dan women who distinguish themselves through generosity and hospitality.

The We Culture

The We live in the forested area of southwestern Ivory Coast and Liberia. Originally subsistence farmers, many We now work in commercial and government jobs. Their traditional culture has many similarities to the Dan, who live near them. The We are known for their abilities as healers who use medicinal plants found in their forest habitat.

They use masks to contact guardian spirits through the spirits of their ancestors. One of the masks they make is called a *gela* mask (the Ancient One). This powerful looking, frightening mask **(figure 5)** is carved of wood and decorated with many attached horns, cowrie shells, fangs, hair, and fiber. The many horns in this particular mask increase its fierceness. The terrifying effect of this mask on an audience can only be imagined. Is this one of the most frightening masks you have ever seen?

The Guro Culture

The Guro live in the savanna and the forests of Ivory Coast. They are a farming society whose main crops are coffee, cotton, rice, cocoa, and yams. They trace their lineage,

Figure 5
We
Gela Mask
(The Ancient One)

through oral histories, back to the Mali Empire of the 13th century. Later they moved south to their present location. Private associations that use masks are an integral part of their culture. The Guro masks are among the most elegantly styled in West Africa.

There is a Guro tradition of three masks that represent various figures. One mask, called *Gu*, is a beautiful, young woman. Another is *Zaouli*, a bearded man, and the third is *Zamble*, an antelope with crocodile or pan-

ther teeth. The Guro wear these masks in dances representing various stories. According to legend, a Guro hunter captured these masks from the bush and was able to harness the magical powers they contain.

This example of Zamble **(figure 6)** is brightly colored with stripes and geometric shapes. The elongated shape of the face is typical of the Guro mask. Many of their other masks are in the form of large animals, such as elephants and buffalo. The Guro use

Figure 6
Guro
Zamble Mask

masks in secret societies and at important public events, such as the enthronement of a leader.

The Benin Culture

The Benin culture dates back several centuries. It reached the height of its power during the 1500s and 1600s. Craftsworkers made

A young man learns the art of wood carving in Benin City, Nigeria.

remarkable pieces of art—many cast in brass, some carved in ivory—for the king and his court. The British overthrew the Benin ruler in 1897, destroyed the royal palace, and imposed a period of colonization. The kingdom of Benin is now part of the state of Nigeria. Many of the people work in farming and timber enterprises.

Both the purpose and criteria of royal art are entirely different from those devoted to the attention of the spirit world. Benin art, sponsored by the court of the king, was designed to support imperial prestige. The king, called the *oba*, was both a political and a spiritual leader. He was thought to be both human and divine. Only the oba could commission works of ivory, bronze, or copper. These pieces of art were made to honor the king and commemorate him in life and death.

Masks were made for ceremonial wear. Sometimes they were worn as a chest piece, on the hip, or as a buckle. This particular mask (**figure 7**) is carved from ivory and is thought to have been worn by the oba over the hip. The delicate, idealized features are characteristic of Benin artwork. A series of faces is carved around the head as a crown and around the neck as a collar. These are the bearded figures of Portuguese traders, who appear as a motif in Benin art. The Portuguese began trade with the Benin in the 15th century.

Figure 7
Benin
Ivory Mask

In Benin, school children attend class, *left,* and dancers perform at the court of the oba, *below.*

A shrine to a Yoruba goddess is located in a sacred grove in Oshogbo, Nigeria.

They increased the wealth of the oba and brought new materials and products into the kingdom.

The Yoruba Culture

The Yoruba are a large ethnic group of more than 20 million people who live in southwestern Nigeria. They trace their ancestry back to the kingdom of Ife, whose height of achievement and power dates back to the period from the 11th to the 15th century.

Although the majority of the Yoruba have converted to Christianity or Islam, the Yoruba traditional religion thrives among its remaining followers. Some of the traditional elements have also been retained by Christian and Muslim converts. In the Yoruba belief system, there are four types of spiritual beings: a supreme god, a group of subordinate gods, deified ancestors, and nature spirits.

The Yoruba society traditionally existed as a group of separate kingdoms. Some of those

Figure 8
Yoruba
Beaded Headdress

in rural areas were centered around agriculture. Some were highly urbanized. For example, the city of Ibadan was one of the largest cities in precolonial Africa. Modern-day Yoruba engage in many occupations. They work as business people, government workers, farmers, laborers, and artisans.

Yoruba artists became skilled at making objects from glass beads that had been introduced by European trade in the 1800s.

Garments and objects were covered with elaborate, colorful, beaded designs. Only a king had the right to wear a beaded crown headdress. This crown **(figure 8)** has a face designed on it. A bird sits at the very top of the crown, gazing down at the king. Strands of beads, a beaded veil, or beaded flaps would hang from the bottom of the crown to cover the king's face. This served to set the king apart from all commoners. The surface of the

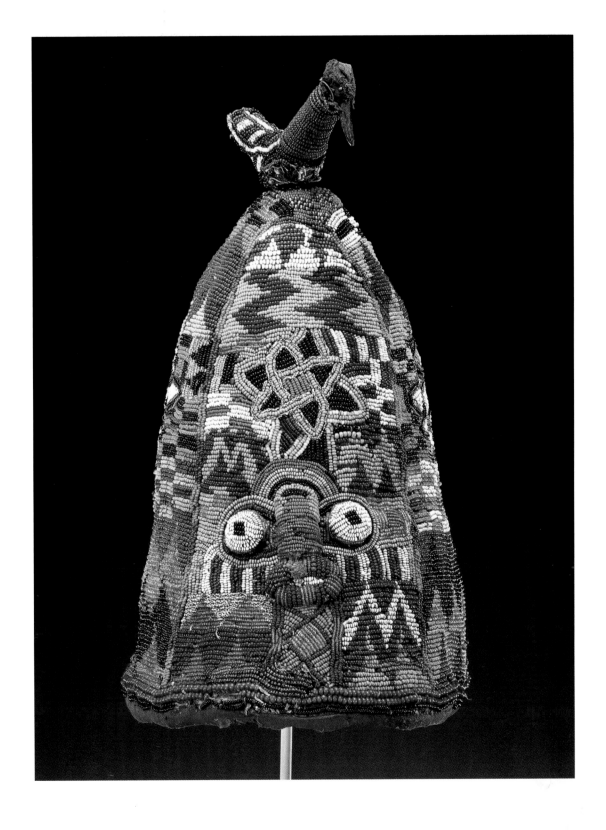

headdress is covered with a variety of zigzag, striped, and other geometric patterns. Yoruba artists are also known for their sculpture made of wood and metal.

The Bamum Culture

Three related ethnic groups, the Bamum, the Bamlike, and the Tikar, live in the grasslands of Cameroon. The grasslands were at one time governed by a king, called a *fon*. According to legend, the fon had the power to transform himself into an animal, such as a leopard, a buffalo, or an elephant. The fon was responsible for officiating at ceremonial and religious functions.

Craftspeople made works of art for the fon. These works included sculpture, masks, thrones, jewelry, and ceremonial costumes. Private societies also had masks that were used for various purposes, such as illustrating and enforcing the society's traditions and celebrating public events.

The Bamum are a relatively small ethnic group. The majority have converted to Islam, and they make their living mainly through farming grains, vegetables, and coffee.

This buffalo mask **(figure 9)** is thought to belong to the *kwifoyn* association of the Bamum culture. The kwifoyn are a high-ranking association responsible for upholding the community's laws and social customs.

A woman participates in an elephant mask festival in Bafoussan, a center for provincial administration in the western highlands of Cameroon, *left*.

Figure 9, Bamum, *Buffalo Mask*

Women work in a maize field in Angola.

Buffalo masks represent strength to the Bamum, and this carved wooden mask does look powerful with its protruding horns, ears, eyes, nostrils, and teeth. The mask is shown with a costume of brown feathers. The buffalo was greatly respected for its strength and intelligence. Can you imagine a dance being performed with this dramatic mask and feather costume? Other animal motifs that appear in grassland art include the spider, the chimpanzee, and the elephant.

Central Africa

Central Africa includes the nations of Gabon, Congo, Chad, Central African Republic, the Democratic Republic of the Congo, and Angola. This region is covered with forests, rain forests, and open and tree-covered savannas. The economies of most cultural groups are traditionally agricultural. The crops include bananas, root vegetables, and grains. In addition, people in this region raise domestic animals and hunt wild game.

Central Africans use masks for coming-of-age ceremonies, initiations into secret societies, funerals, healing, and ancestor worship.

The Bakwele Culture

The Bakwele people live in northern Gabon and along the border of Congo. They are mainly subsistence farmers, and little is known about their traditional culture and religious beliefs.

They are known for a gorilla mask they make—called *gon*—and for their abstract, often heart-shaped masks. This Bakwele mask (**figure 10**) shows a heart-shaped face framed by curved horns that also form a heart shape. The eyes are thin slits and the nose is shaped

Figure 10, Bakwele, *Heart-Shaped Mask*

48

like a triangle. Other features of this design are eyelike motifs on the top of each horn. Portions of this area have been painted white. The Bakwele use the gorilla mask to exert authority and power, but they use this type of heart-shaped mask for initiation ceremonies and at the conclusion of a period of mourning.

The Teke Culture

The Teke live in Congo and eastern Gabon. They raise vegetables and bananas and hunt wild game. In their traditional belief system, there is a supreme god, called *Nzami*, and several ancestor and nature spirits. Village chieftains have authority over local communities. The king, who has the greatest authority, is considered to be both human and divine. He appeals to the spiritual forces on behalf of the Teke people.

The Teke make fetishes for spiritual and protective purposes. Fetishes are small statues—some small enough to be handheld—used to ensure luck in hunting, fertility, and health. Sometimes the fetishes might be filled with magical substances.

The Tsaye, a subgroup within the Teke culture, make a distinctive disc-shaped mask. This wooden mask **(figure 11)** is boldly geometric and abstract in design. Masks of this type are often painted in combinations of red, white, brown, blue, and black. Geometric shapes define the eyes, nose, and mouth. Other shapes on the mask are thought to represent the sky, half-moon, and stars. The mask is worn with a costume made of raffia

This dirt road is the main route through Central African Republic.

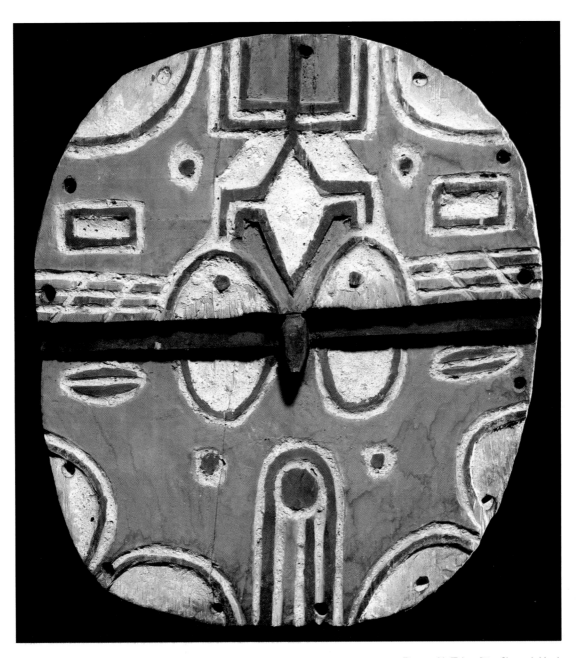

Figure 11, Teke, *Disc-Shaped Mask*

Figure 12
Pende
Panya Ngombe Mask

fabric and feathers and is used by a secret society. The person wearing the mask performs for the community at important events, such as the weddings and funerals of high-ranking individuals.

The Pende Culture

The Pende live in the Democratic Republic of the Congo (formerly Zaire) and the Central African Republic. They were a major group in central Africa at one time, but in the last century, their population has declined. They are known for their artistic skill.

The Pende make refined masks. Some are life-size for use in performances, some are very small masks for use as protective amulets, and some are large masks for use as architectural elements on buildings. The masks represent ancestors, human characters, animals, or a combination of these things. This Pende mask **(figure 12)**, called *panya ngombe*, is thought to be a combination of a wild cow and a human. This type of mask is used in coming-of-age ceremonies for young men. Because of its size, this mask may have been made as an interior decorative piece for a high-ranking person's house. It is made of wood and painted with geometric shapes. The Pende also make pottery and do metal work. They are particularly known for their small, carved ivory whistles and pendants.

The Kuba Culture

The Kuba live in the south central part of the Democratic Republic of the Congo. They trace the history of their kingdom back through the reigns of more than 100 kings. In the 16th century, the Kuba were a powerful group that controlled some of the trade routes in central Africa. Modern-day Kuba live in urban areas and work in a wide range of occupations. In the rural areas, most Kuba grow grains, fruits, and vegetables, and they hunt and fish.

The Kuba believe in a supreme being called *Nyeem*, who created the world. Nature spirits and important ancestors can be called upon by humans to ensure fertility, health, and success in hunting. *Woot* is the legendary founder of the Kuba people and their first king.

The Kuba make three important masks that illustrate their legendary history. One of these is the *Ngady Amwaash* mask **(figure 13)**. This mask represents Woot's sister. It is a helmet mask, which means that it covers the entire head of the wearer. It is carved in wood, then decorated in a mainly triangular pattern with red, yellow, white, and black paint. (The

Figure 13
Kuba, *Ngady Amwaash Mask*

Village life in this rural area of the Democratic Republic of the Congo is isolated. Almost no traffic passes through the region.

pattern of painted triangles is also used in Kuba textile designs.) The lines coming down from the eyes represent tears. Blue and white beads form the outlines of the eyebrows, nose, mouth, forehead, and top of the head. Cowrie shells cover the head, and colored fabric covers the ears.

The other two masks that illustrate Kuba legendary history are called *Mwaash aMbooy* and *Bwoom*. Mwaash aMbooy represents the king, possibly Woot, and Bwoom represents the king's brother or other high-ranking Kuba. These masks are used at initiation rites, ceremonial events, and funerals.

The Kuba place great importance on the artistic appearance of objects and clothing. They make a range of objects decorated with beads and shells and extraordinary beadwork-and-shell costumes that cover the wearer from head to foot in a dazzling design of color and pattern. They are also famous for their fine woven and appliquéd textiles.

The Lega Culture

The Lega, who live in the northeastern part of the Democratic Republic of the Congo, are a farming, hunting, and fishing culture. They are known for their carvings—including masks—in wood and ivory. Participation in an association, called *Bwami*, is an important element of Lega life. The Lega strive to advance to higher and higher levels in the Bwami association by acquiring knowledge and exhibiting moral excellence. Bwami has four or seven grades, depending on the particular Lega group. Masks are used as emblems to signify a person's rank in the Bwami association. They are worn during initiations and other ceremonies, held in the hands, or displayed with other masks in groups.

This Lega mask **(figure 14)** is from the *kindi* level, the highest rank of Bwami. The wooden mask is very simple and elegant in design. Lega masks are painted white, which

Figure 14
Lega
Bwami Mask

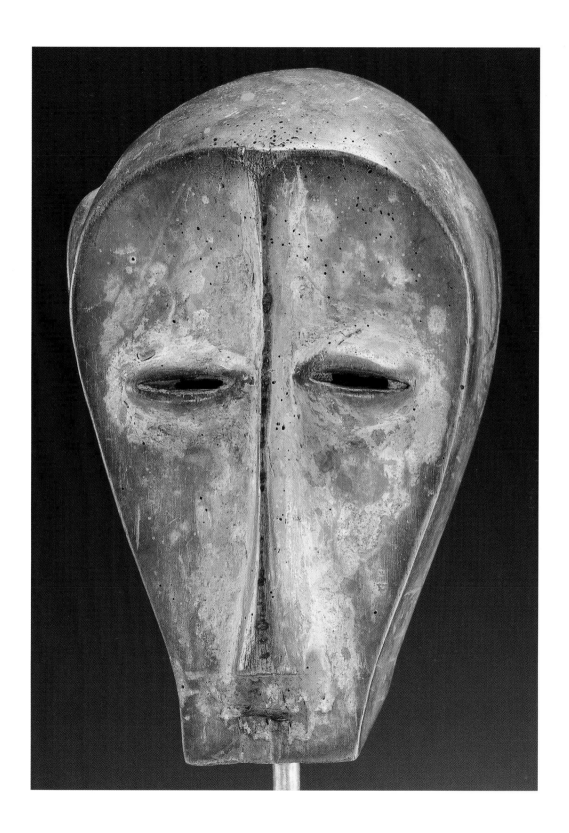

Figure 15
Chokwe
Mwana Pwo
Mask

gives them a ghostlike appearance. The most common Bwami mask is a small wooden face with a beard attached to it. Only the two highest grades have ivory objects as emblems of rank. The senior kindi—those who instruct the younger kindi initiates—also wear a hat of cowrie shells and elephant-tail hairs. Masks and other emblems are passed on to other members of the association as they are initiated into the various grades.

The Chokwe Culture

More than one million Chokwe people live in the Democratic Republic of the Congo, Angola, and Zambia. They continue to resist outside intervention and retain a strong connection to their traditional customs and belief system. Some Chokwe people have gone to work as laborers in factories and copper mines, but most live in small villages and are not united under a single ruler. They farm, herd cattle, and hunt game. The crops they raise include millet, cassava (a plant grown for its edible roots), peanuts, yams, and maize. The Chokwe are known for their large sculptured figures of ancestors, masks, baskets, and elaborate jewelry made of copper, tin, wood, or stone.

The Chokwe believe in a supreme being called *Nzambi*, who created the universe but is uninvolved in current events. The spirits of ancestors and natural forces are the important guardians of human beings on earth. Private associations also play an important role in the Chokwe culture.

One of these private groups—the *Makanda* association—uses a group of masks in its coming-of-age ceremonies for young men. One of these masks **(figure 15)** is a *Mwana Pwo*, a maiden mask that represents a female ancestor. This type of mask portrays the ideal

of female beauty. Here, the eyes of the smoothly carved face are decorated with gold. A tattooed pattern gracefully curves around the eyes to the cheeks. Gold earrings adorn the ears, and the hair is made of delicately woven fiber. The effect is one of elegant serenity. The Chokwe also use three masks representing male ancestors in the coming-of-age ceremonies.

The Songhay Culture

The Songhay are an ethnic group of 1.5 million people who live in the Democratic Republic of the Congo. They are related to the Luba, who live near them. Secret associations are an important part of the Songhay culture.

Among other things, the associations are responsible for conveying Songhay history, legends, and rules of behavior.

In the Songhay language, a mask is a *kifwebe*. Secret associations use masks in initiation ceremonies, in ceremonies honoring current or ancestral leaders, and in ceremonies welcoming important guests.

This mask **(figure 16)** shows the highly geometric design Songhay sculptors use when carving a kifwebe. A square shape defines the mouth and chin. A triangle is used to make the nose, and ovals form the eyes. Curved lines are cut into the mask and painted. The predominance of white signifies that a mask is female. Male masks have more red and black. The curved lines decorating the mask

Figure 16
Songhay
Face Mask

Figure 17
Luba
Kifwebe Mask

are thought to represent animal stripes. Magical substances can be attached to the top of the mask, which give it great power, and a costume can be attached to the holes along the side and bottom of the mask.

Songhay artists also make amulets (charms) and "power statues" that protect the owner from illness and calamities. Some of these carved wooden figures are heavily decorated with feathers, beads, animal fur, and metal.

The Luba Culture

The Luba also live in the Democratic Republic of the Congo, near the Songhay people. Their population amounts to more than one million. Farming is the Luba's main economic activity, and maize and millet are the most important crops.

The Luba trace their settlement back to the 8th century and their kingdom back to King Kalala Ilunga of the 16th century. The king had absolute authority and was thought to be both human and divine. Women figure prominently in Luba myth, and they held important positions in the Luba royal court. Children, too, are highly valued in Luba society.

Artists also occupy a high place in Luba society, and some are thought to be knowledgeable about magic. Among the objects artists make are amulets, masks, and sculptures portraying women.

The Luba make a mask similar to the Songhay mask (see figure 16 on page 57), and they also call it a kifwebe. This mask (**figure 17**) is shaped like a sphere and is characteristic of the Luba style. It has curved lines cut into the wood around the eyes, forehead, and cheeks. These grooves are painted white. Woven fiber sometimes hangs down from the mask, representing hair. The mask is used during funerals and ceremonies honoring ancestors. Masks are also used in many theatrical performances.

60

Other African masks include a wood and metal Ndomo mask of the Bamana people in Mali, *opposite page, left;* a Baoule snake and hyena mask from Mali, *opposite page, right;* and a Dan Deangle mask from northern Liberia and western Ivory Coast, *above.*

Conclusion

THE MASKS OF AFRICA WERE MADE PRIMARILY for religious and ritual purposes that have no parallel in European-based societies. The masks were not meant to be decorative objects or museum pieces, but were made to be used in public performances and private rituals.

Information on the culture and traditions of African ethnic groups is incomplete and, in some cases, nonexistent. Much of the traditional way of life has now disappeared in Africa because of the spread of Islam and Christianity and the effect of colonial rule. In the 1800s and much of the 1900s, Africa was dominated by European powers. The French, British, Belgian, German, Italian, Dutch, and Portuguese colonists divided much of the land and controlled most of Africa. The borders the Europeans made split up some societies and grouped others together. Ghana did not gain independence from colonial occupation until 1957. After that, a wave of independence movements followed throughout the continent. The aftermath of colonial rule and subsequent revolution have left many African societies struggling for survival and stability.

The art of mask making survives in some societies that still make them for private rituals and public ceremonies. Carvers in some places make masks especially for tourists and collectors. All are worthy of further study.

For Further Reading

Cameroon in Pictures. Minneapolis: Lerner Publications Company, 1992.

Central African Republic in Pictures. Minneapolis: Lerner Publications Company, 1996.

Cote D'Ivoire in Pictures. Minneapolis: Lerner Publications Company, 1988.

Kenya in Pictures. Minneapolis: Lerner Publications Company, 1991.

Liberia in Pictures. Minneapolis: Lerner Publications Company, 1988.

Mali in Pictures. Minneapolis: Lerner Publications Company, 1990.

Nigeria in Pictures. Minneapolis: Lerner Publications Company, 1995.

Senegal in Pictures. Minneapolis: Lerner Publications Company, 1989.

Zaire in Pictures. Minneapolis: Lerner Publications Company, 1992.

Selected Bibliography

Biondi Joann, and Jim Haskins. *From Afar to Zulu: A Dictionary of African Cultures*. New York: Walker and Co., 1995.

Crowder, Michael, and Roland Oliver. *The Cambridge Encyclopedia of Africa*. Cambridge: Cambridge University Press, 1981.

Kerchache, Jacques, Jean-Louis Paudrat, and Lucien Stephan. *Art of Africa*. New York: Harry N. Abrams, Inc., 1993.

Murray, Jocelyn, ed. *Cultural Atlas of Africa*. New York: Facts on File, 1989.

Olson, James S. *The Peoples of Africa: An Ethnohistorical Dictionary*. Westport, Connecticut: Greenwood Press, 1996.

Phillips, Tom, ed. *Africa: The Art of a Continent*. New York: Prestel, 1995.

Segy, Ladislas. *Masks of Black Africa*. New York: Dover Publications, 1976.

Index

About the Author

Carol Finley studied art history at Northwestern University and did graduate work at Bryn Mawr College. She worked as a trader in the financial markets before pursuing a career in writing. She lives in London and New York City.

Photo Acknowledgments

Brooklyn Museum of Art, Gift of Dr. and Mrs. Abbott Lippman, late 19th-early 20th century, Wood, pigment, 13¼" H x 11½" W x 4" D (33.5 x 29.3 x 11.5 cm), 49; Buffalo Museum of Science C12963, 29; Photograph © 1998 Founders Society Purchase, Eleanor Clay Ford Fund for African Art, The Detroit Institute of Arts, Accession No. 79.37, Pende Mask, *Panya Ngombe Mask*, 1875/1925 - African H 21.59 W 52.07 D 16.51, 50; © Victor Englebert, 12 (left), 20 (bottom), 23, 40 (top); Werner Forman/ Art Resource, NY, 11 (detail), 60, 61; Giraudon/Art Resource, NY, 15; © Dave G. Houser, 28 (bottom left); © Wolfgang Kaehler, 19 (detail); © Jason Laure, 46, 48, 52; © 1983 The Metropolitan Museum of Art, The Michael C. Rockefeller Memorial Collection, Gift of Nelson A. Rockefeller, 1964. (1978.412.435-.436), 25; © 1998 The Metropolitan Museum of Art, The Michael C. Rockefeller Memorial Collection, Bequest of Nelson A. Rockefeller, 1979. (1979.206.196), 27; © 1986 The Metropolitan Museum of Art, Gift of Lillian and Sidney Lichter, 1985. (1985.420.2), Photograph by Schecter Lee, 33; © 1998 The Metropolitan Museum of Art, The Michael C. Rockefeller Memorial Collection, Bequest of Nelson A. Rockefeller, 1979. (1979.206.105), 37; © 1981 The Metropolitan Museum of Art, The Michael C. Rockefeller Memorial Collection, Gift of Nelson A. Rockefeller, 1972. (1978.412.323), Photograph by Jerry L. Thompson, 2 and 39; © 1993 The Metropolitan Museum of Art, The Michael C. Rockefeller Memorial Collection, Bequest of Nelson A. Rockefeller, 1979. (1979.206.8), 47; © 1991 The Metropolitan Museum of Art, The Michael C. Rockefeller Memorial Collection, Bequest of Nelson A. Rockefeller, 1979. (1979.206.83), 57; National Museum of African Art, Eliot Elisofon Photographic Archives, Smithsonian Institution, Photograph by Franko Khoury, 55; The Newark Museum/Art Resource, NY, 16; Panos Pictures: © Fred Hoogervorst, 26, © J. H. Morris, 38 and 40 (bottom), © Betty Press, 5 (detail), 12–13 (center) and 41, © David Reed, 8 and 17, © Liba Taylor, 30; *Gela Mask (The Ancient One)*, "The Seattle Art Museum," Gift of Katherine White & the Boeing Co." Photo: Paul Macapia, 35; *Kifwebe Mask*, "The Seattle Art Museum," Gift of Katherine White and the Boeing Co., Photo: Susan Dirk, 59; TRIP/M. Jelliffe, 20 (upper left); TRIP/H. Hockey, 44; © Brian A. Vikander, 7 (detail), 20 (middle right), 28 (upper right), 31, 60 (right); © Virginia Museum of Fine Arts, Richmond VA. The Adolph D. and Wilkins C. Williams Fund. Yoruba Culture (Nigeria, Republic of Benin), *Crown*, Glass bead, cloth, string, 19"H x 6¾" W (48.2 x 17.2 cm), photos by Katherine Wetzel, 42 (detail) and 43; © Virginia Museum of Fine Arts, Richmond, VA. The Arthur and Margaret Glasgow Fund. Bamum Culture (Cameroon, Detail, *Buffalo Mask and Feather Costume*, Wood, feathers, burlap, string, Mask: 7½"H x 16"W x 29"D (19 x 40.6 x 73.6 cm), Costume: 48"H x 38"W, (122 x 96.5 cm), photo by Katherine Wetzel, 45; © Virginia Museum of Fine Arts, Richmond, VA. The Arthur and Margaret Glasgow Fund. Photo: Katherine Wetzel. © Virginia Museum of Fine Arts, Kuba Culture (Zaire), *Ngady Amwaash Mask*, Wood, paint, cloth, cowrie shells, glass beads, string, 12½"H x 8"W x 9½"D (31.7 x 20.3 x 24.1 cm), 51; © Virginia Museum of Fine Arts, Richmond, VA. The Arthur and Margaret Glasgow Fund. Lega Culture (Eastern Zaire), *Bwami Mask*, Wood, white clay, 10"H x 6"W x 3¼"D (25.4 x 15.2 x 8.3 cm), photo by Katherine Wetzel, 53; Laura Westlund, 14 (drawing), 22 (map).

Front Cover: © Virginia Museum of Fine Arts, Richmond, VA. The Arthur and Margaret Glasgow Fund, Kuba Culture (Zaire), *Ngady Amwaash Mask*, wood, paint, cloth cowrie shells, glass beads, string, 12½" H x 8"W x 9¼"D (31.7 x20.3 x24.1 cm), photo by Katherine Wetzel.

Back cover: Photograph © 1998 Founders Society Purchase, Eleanor Clay Ford Fund for African Art, The Detroit Institute of Arts, Accession No. 79.37, Pende Mask, *Panya Ngombe Mask*, 1875/1925 - African H 21.59 W 52.07 D 16.51.